The Nature Kid's Guide to
MOUNTAIN GOATS

DAVID ANDERSON

LP Media Inc. Publishing

For information address LP Media Inc. Publishing,
30012 Variolite St NW, Princeton MN 55371
www.lpmedia.org

Publication Data

Mountain Goats
The Nature Kid's Guide to Mountain Goats — First edition.

Summary: "Learn all about Mountain Goats, the Nature Kid Way"
— Provided by publisher.

ISBN: 979-8-89818-167-3

[1. Mountain Goats – Non-Fiction] I. Title.

Title: The Nature Kid's Guide to Mountain Goats

CONTENTS

ROCKY HEIGHTS

Howl! Wind sweeps across the mountain. A mountain goat climbs higher.

Mountain goats live in high places up to 13,000 feet tall. They make their homes on rocky cliffs and steep slopes. Up there, the air is thin and cold. Strong winds can blow up to 100 miles per hour.

These goats need rough, rocky ground. Their special hooves grip the rocks tightly. Staying on steep cliffs helps them avoid predators.

Winters are harsh in their mountain homes. Snow covers the ground for six months. Temperatures can drop to 50 degrees below zero. Mountain goats survive where few other animals can live.

PEAK PLACES

Brrrr! Cold air rushes by. A mountain goat stands tall against the wind.

Mountain goats live only in North America. They roam the Rocky Mountains from Montana to Alaska. Washington and Idaho have mountain goats too.

These goats like living at high **altitudes**. In summer, they climb even higher to find food.

During winter months, mountain goats move lower. They find spots with less snow and where there is still grass to eat.

Mountain goats were brought to Colorado in 1947. They did not live there before that!

SIZE UP

Peek! A large male mountain goat looks down the cliff.

Mountain goats may look fluffy, but they are big and strong. Males can weigh up to 300 pounds, about as heavy as your refrigerator!

Females weigh about half that, around 150 pounds.

Standing about 3 to 3.5 feet tall at the shoulder, a mountain goat would be a little shorter than most 2nd graders. And from nose to tail they are 5 to 6 feet long, about as long as your bed!

A mountain goat's beard can grow up to 7 inches long! Males and females both have them.

BUILT TOUGH

DID YOU KNOW?
Mountain goat horns are made of keratin. That is the same stuff as your fingernails!

Shiver! It's freezing cold on the mountain. But the goat stands warm under his fur coat.

Mountain goats have amazing bodies built for cold, rocky places. Their thick white fur has two layers. The outer layer keeps water and wind out. The inner layer traps heat close to their skin.

Their hooves are like built-in climbing shoes. Each hoof has a hard outer edge and a soft, rubbery pad. The pad grips rock like a sneaker sole.

Mountain goats have short, pointed horns. Both males (billies) and females (nannies) grow them. These horns never fall off. They keep growing the goat's whole life!

SUPER SENSES

Sniff! A mountain goat sniffs the air. He smells food buried under snow!

Mountain goats have amazing eyesight. Their eyes sit on the sides of their head, so they can see almost everything around them without turning.

Their hearing is sharp too. Mountain goats can hear the crunch of a predator's footstep from far away, even in howling wind.

They also have a strong sense of smell. It helps them find food buried under snow and tells them when other goats are nearby.

Mountain goats can see the colors blue and yellow, but can not see red!

STAYING SAFE

Perch! Mountain goat stands on a narrow ledge. She's safe here.

Mountain goats have many ways to stay safe from predators. Their white fur helps them blend in with the snow. Predators have a hard time seeing them on snowy cliffs.

Their sharp horns are good for defense. Both males and females use them to fight off enemies. A quick jab can scare away a hungry predator.

But their best defense is climbing. They can hide on small mountain ledges that no other animal can get to!

Mountain goat mothers will charge a full-grown grizzly bear to protect their babies!

15

GRASSY GRUB

Chirp! Birds sing as a mountain goat munches fresh green grass.

Mountain goats eat mostly plants. They munch on grasses, herbs, and mosses. In summer, they find lots of green food on mountain meadows.

In winter, food is harder to find. They eat dried grasses and shrubs. They also nibble on **lichen** growing on rocks.

Mountain goats spend about nine hours eating each day. They need lots of food to stay warm in the cold mountains.

Mountain goats even lick rocks to get salt and minerals!

GOAT TALK

A mother mountain goat can find her baby by its unique call, even in a herd of many goats!

Bleat! A goat bellows a call. She's talking to her herd.

Mountain goats are generally quiet but can make grunts, bleats, and snorts. Kids bleat to call their mothers. Mothers bleat back so their babies can find them. Males make low grunts during mating season.

Goats also talk with their bodies. A goat may lower its head to show it is angry. They stamp their feet to threaten rivals or predators.

Mountain goats use scent to communicate too. They have special glands near their horns. These glands leave a smell on rocks and trees, which other goats can read like messages.

WATCH OUT

Growl! A mountain lion stalks the herd. The goats sprint away.

Mountain goats have many predators. Mountain lions are their main threat. These big cats hunt goats on steep cliffs.

Golden eagles swoop down to catch young kids. Wolves and bears also hunt mountain goats when they can.

Most predators hunt in lower areas. The high cliffs are safer. Predators cannot climb the steep rocks where goats live.

Mountain lions can leap up to 40 feet to catch prey! They hide and jump from above.

QUICK
ESCAPE

Thump! The mountain goat leaps away in a flash! It races downhill.

Mountain goats escape danger by climbing. They run up and down steep cliffs where predators cannot follow. Their hooves grip tiny ledges that other animals miss.

This speed helps them survive. A mountain goat can climb 1,500 feet in about 20 minutes.

Kids stay close to their mothers during escapes. When one goat runs, others follow quickly to safety.

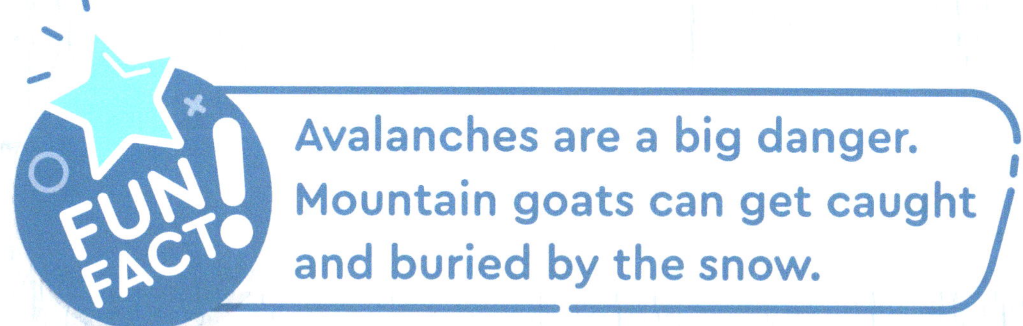

Avalanches are a big danger. Mountain goats can get caught and buried by the snow.

CLIFF CLIMBERS

Clack! Hooves hit the rocky ledge. A mountain goat jumps up.

Mountain goats are amazing climbers. They can walk on cliffs that are almost straight up and down. Their hooves have rough pads that grip rock like rubber.

These goats jump from ledge to ledge with ease. A single leap can carry them up to 12 feet!

Mountain goats place each step just right. If they miss their spot they could fall all the way down the mountain.

Mountain goats can climb slopes as steep as 60 degrees. That is almost straight up!

DAY LIFE

Yawn! Morning light hits the rocky ledge. A mountain goat wakes up.

Mountain goats are **diurnal**, which means they are active during the day. They rest at night on rocky ledges.

Mornings are busy times. Goats spend hours eating grass and plants. They graze in meadows and along cliff sides.

Afternoons are for resting. Goats lie down to chew their cud. They also watch for danger.

As evening comes, goats find safe sleeping spots on high ledges.

Mountain goats take dust baths. Rolling in dirt helps keep bugs away from their fur and skin!

HERD HANGOUT

Click, clack! A herd of mountain goats gather on the rocks together.

Mountain goats live in herds. A herd usually has 4 to 20 goats. Females and young goats stay together most of the year. Living in a group helps them stay safe because more eyes means more chances to spot danger.

Nanny goats lead the herd. The oldest females decide where to go and pick the safest paths.

Male goats, called billies, often live alone. They join herds at certain times of year.

Mountain goats can be aggressive. They often fight each other to show who is the boss.

BATTLING BILLIES

Jab! Two billies circle and clash on the rocky cliff.

Fall is mating season for mountain goats. This time is called the rut. It happens from November to December.

Male goats compete for females. Billies dig pits and paw the dirt to show off.

Two billies may fight over a female. They circle each other slowly, then jab their sharp horns at each other's sides and rump. Their skin is extra thick there to protect them from these stabs!

The strongest billy wins the right to mate.

Billies can lose over 50 pounds during mating season from all the fighting and chasing!

CUTE KIDS

DID YOU KNOW?
Kids can stand and walk within minutes of being born. They must keep up with mom on steep cliffs!

Hop! A fluffy kid leaps across a spring mountain meadow.

Baby mountain goats are called kids. Most nannies have just one kid at a time. But sometimes they have twins.

Kids are born in spring, around May or June. These newborns weigh about 6 to 7 pounds.

Baby goats have white fur from birth. Their coats are soft and fluffy. Kids are born without horns, but small black nubs start poking through within just a few weeks.

They start climbing on rocks at only one day old! Mothers will walk below their kids on steep slopes so they can catch them if they slip.

NANNY CARE

DID YOU KNOW?

If a kid wanders too far away, its mother will call it back with a soft bleating sound.

Step, step, jump! A baby goat follows its mother up the mountain. Every step is a lesson!

Nanny goats are caring mothers. They feed their kids rich milk for about 3 to 4 months.

Mothers teach their young to climb. Kids follow close behind their moms. This is how they learn which rocks are safe.

Nannies protect their babies from danger. They stand between kids and predators. A mother will even charge at threats.

Young goats stay with mom for about one year. Then they are ready to live on their own.

ANCIENT CLIMBERS

Crunch. Long ago, mountain goats walked from Asia to North America on a bridge of ice.

Mountain goats didn't always live in America. They **migrated** from Asia about 40,000 years ago during the Ice Age.

The goats that climbed highest lived the longest. Over time, their bodies changed. Their hooves grew two toes that spread wide. Their bones got thick to keep them steady.

They grew big lungs for thin air. They grew a double coat that works in 50 below zero. The mountains shaped them into the tough climbers they are today.

HELPING HERDS

Some mountain goats wear tiny radio collars so scientists can follow where they go all year long!

Whirr! A helicopter hovers over a snowy peak. A mountain goat looks up from a rocky ledge.

Mountain goat herds are getting smaller. The climate is warming. Snow covers their food. Heat pushes them higher, but they are already near the top.

People are helping. Some goats are relocated to mountain ranges where more goats were needed.

Scientists track goat families with radio collars. They even use DNA from goat droppings to learn how herds are doing.

GLOSSARY

altitudes
How high up a place is from the ground.

migrate
To move from one place to another.

keratin
The hard material that makes up horns and fingernails.

lichen
A flat, crusty plant that grows on rocks and trees.

diurnal
Active during the day and sleeping at night.